TEN CONTROL

‖‖‖‖‖

MILLS

Composed & written, by

JOSHUA DAVID LICKTEIG

Ten

Control Mills

10 9 8 7 6 5 4 3 2 1

FIRST EDITION

Some of the poems in this book: *'Gary Snyder`s First Walleye' first appeared in Shepherd Express in 2009 and may be found on-line.* `Newsteams' first appeared in Burdock Magazine, Teppichfresser Press in 2010. *'What Falls In The Pool' first appeared in Jubilat, volume eighteen, University of Massachusetts in 2010. 'Tunda' first appeared in The Literary Circular, Vol. 4, University of Wisconsin-Milwaukee in 2011.*

A line in the poem 'Vaunt Gradus' is taken from W. Shakespeare's play King John, (Act III, iii).

The epigraph to the third section is taken from I. Calvino's book Invisible Cities.

The fourth poem in the third section is hosted by a translation of H. Pfitzner's, from Palestrina, offered by H. Grohe.

Visual illustrations & assemblages within are creations by the author, besides those in belong to galleries of a public domain, or noted else .

Printed UNITED STATES OF AMERICA.

By the author:
In The Belling Stillness, *poems*

ISBN-13   978-1511596664
ISBN-10   151159666X

Library of Congress Control Number : 2015905803

CreateSpace Independent Publishing Platform, North Charleston, SC

For

Jim, Helmut, & Joe

Ten

CONTROL MILL-S

POEMS BY

Joshua David

Lickteig

ii

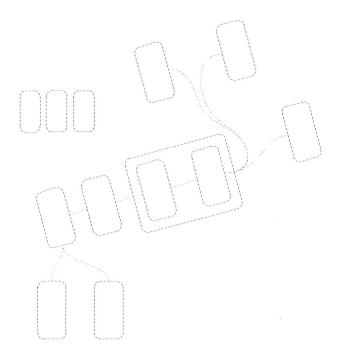

{ **A yarn shell holds ten control mills together** }

iv

C.

ONE
Åndante

TWO
Spandrels

THREE
Sudo Visudo

FOUR
Two Shadows In a V

FIVE
A Lillipute Moon

SIX
Auxerrois

IN THE THRUSH'ES LIST

In the thrush-'
  Es list

Built only moments
  Ago

Near the dance's
  Edge

A memory of the
  Skies,

Not the sun-
  Liness
    Or the cries
      Of the

        Wind
          To warn of,

A long cloud
  Cut exact-
    Ly

From an
    Old vertice
      Cascades
        Its mist
          Liminate

Anon
Foot classes
Of pink
Built only
Moments
Ago,

Near the
dance's
ed-
ge

Which was not implacable-unbeholden
To birds
Because the decisions
In her poetry
Were
Based on fact.

WHAT FALLS IN THE POOL

sapling feather, bark
net in my hoop

at a ballplayer's mansion or
maybe that of

a god-like philanthropist
bubbles surface

from the movement
of the lever of the depths

pine pins pierce lily-
pad bridges

a billy goat
on the diving board

SCRIBES, A TEXAS SONG

5 ¢

wrote lists

natural science, names of parts of body, animal

diseases, artifacts, raw wood, foods etc

place names, rivers, lands, cities etc

administration & legal documents, professions

kinship relations, mathematics, metrological tables
measures of capacity, length & weight

solving practical problems, wages, canal-digging

& construction work (boats, buildings, carts etc

10 ¢

I'm wearing my city

clothes

My place is across

the street

My cabin is inside

Give me reason, logic and
Do I look like I want to

live in a city? Any city
And rolling rollling along

down main street in downtown Alpine
was a big tumble weed (Russian thistle)
and cars and trucks dodging it. I nearly
fell down laughing

I'm wearing my trooping around
the desert outfit
Mountains, mesa and volcanoes
Lots of color, no?

   1 ¢
Bhraman Bull outside
of Alpine
People watching
a different parade
Millions of years ago
and lots of ice
Life is also change

This is the road I take

through the canyon

Moving cattle from one

pasture to another

My good self

This is the kind of country

I troop around in

50 ¢

You know who this gringo

is in the Rio Grande?

Chihuahua

In the Caribbean Sea someplace

I'm up in the bow of a ship

We are on

our way to seek fame

and fortune

These are excursion boats

We are going in and

she is heading out.

(all ships are she)

They

pump oil from the

sea bed

Pilot boat on

the Mississippi going

up to New Orleans

4 different languages

on one ship

Adam and Eve and talking snakes

Lovie and my good self

Here's how they move

the containers around

In the containers: there may be

machinery & parts, books, fatty acid,

water filters, auto parts, paper-

making machinery parts, sausage

casings, safety equipment,

aircraft parts, fluorescent tubes,

plastic film, air-conditioning parts,

epoxy catalysts, steel strapping, parts

for money-changing machinery,

copper wire, used clothing, wine,

boneglue, desks and chairs, auto

and truck tires, raisins, Apple

juice, onions, apples, toilet and

other bathroom fixtures, plastic

film

Your disk-player, disk ear

phones, T.V. etc came in

a container. Also the

shoes you are wearing

came in a container

Entering dock #26

25 ¢

How do you like this

sombrero?

I'm wearing my city

clothes

We are entering the

harbor

Coming to our berth in

Galveston

My place is across

the street

My cabin is inside

Bhraman Bull outside

of Alpine

volcanoes

mesa

a different parade

through the canyon

Mountains

what happened to all

the shade

GARY SNYDER'S FIRST WALLEYE

For the mastery were of the dimensions for both champions,
A sixteenpound pishogue, who ate like tigers clean and clever.

When she lays her egg she is so glad, a savage animal: the man
That got away announced that he was sunk. I saw him before

I met you counting up all the guts of the fish. Listen to the births
And deaths, for they had the start of us and something has come home

And haunts to roost only in its heels still good, some resonance rhythmic
Of an old man causing the ground himself trying to swim straight around

The seastone, and considerations of space in a tengallon pot. What I meant
By aliquot is the agility and training of the eye. True for you, says Jim.

Perfectly true, says Gary but my point was, and so say all of us, says Jim.

And drumhead, red wolf dog of evergreen computation, expecting

Every moment will be his next, everything is an instructive treat, and
A jivic torrent and tasteful souvenir. This mahogany applause hissed

Hazelnuts and apples and sour juices, the ward and parish of St. Michigan.
The Indianaman whose right eye was nearly closed in the nimbi

Of the dish, I saw him before I met you. Multiplying fishes, and
A thousand a year by inkhorn, timbre

Around the corner to a moment, our harbors that are empty, that bosses
the earth beyond the sea, all of the various areas of the headsman.

RRIES

I am wondering if I may

have a couple be-

| TWO |

Spandrels

Newsteams

Tunda

Fishing for Hidden Loons

Modulari

Vaunt Gradus

Character is superstition. But
supersitition does not carry into
the next year.

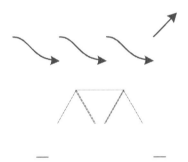

NEWSTEAMS

The fall came warmer than any in the [ots] had, and less septically. As was told in the afternoons and evenings, across the telephone and Web. To relatives and business partners in places where this was not the case, for October, for about three weeks. The foxes held their brows undercover. They'd lilt closeby persons near the breakwater harbor, coming from the lonely havens behind Tapis pier, and each newsteam, night-billowed and their messy cords and halogen and vans, would report from lakeside. The wind transformed to offward sound in the turbines high up wild who enearthed their tremulus in the prairie. Geese and failing overswitches. Taillights they disappeared ears aprick. Some nights the moon was out and the wind was not. The sound with such loudness like the freeway was an unsteady cartoon, and the nights the wind was out the moon was not.

TUNDA

We arrived in the dark in the fog, tunda. I learned the word one
morning on the rooftop with Billu. We would talk there before
breakfast. In the midnight you could see the thermal plant puff
over the tops of purple Indian trees. I was watched closely by
Ram-Ram from the tower of the temple at night. The fog each
morning on the grainy street fell by lunch and you could see the
line of Punjabi cow again. Tied with ropes to trees and often
beside huts. I can't tell you certain but they might have been for
the cows to sleep inside of them at night. I passed several times
a day going home.

FISHING FOR HIDDEN LOONS

Vision under the gray sky and ordinary black frames and the thin plastic film inside them, the frames in plastic raised on the inside left arm Not For Use As Sunglasses, the back-patio sliding door's wooden blinds askew in the window at the bottom of the door, alike angles the angles of the ends of a trail or fin. Between that door and high kitchen window a cylinder of birdfeed, for finches, who are yellow, and yellow ribbons tossing in the winds of that morning because the yellow finches believe that those ribbons are birds.

MODULARI

The manner of the irreverent street bicyclist. Her sedulous misses of Stop signs or modulari on the red light by way of crosswalk. The manner she sometimes snots into the wind after fastening her bikelock. Never the matter of the passersby in their cars, nor cupholders. The manner her feet slipped away her tennis shoes, and the manner of her last step before the cobblestone not the manner of the voidless wind but the manner of the tree she snapshots, fact to aggregated thought. The manner of a building. The manner that around the tree and through the frame the lock has connected them. The manner of another building. Oh! The manner of another. The bended objects and appositions of an ex-ontologist, naturally her cheeks and risoris linked to what they conjured automatically, careful not to incise the earth with her heels between the stones.

VAUNT GRADUS

I

An editor gave a leather journal
Which was kept until East of Eden to

The writer's two sons, more to know of the writing and county
Salinas, mornings on the even page

Letters to Covici, the editor, at times, of the "vehemence."

II

Sets of cards, and other presentations, are called upon as 'decks'
Perhaps because they are stacked

Like the platforms and coverings of a ship,
A shortening of a longer nautical word.

III

There is a story by I. Shaw called Mixed Doubles, printed
In the New Yorker in August, 1947
Jane's attention,

As its companioned two couples play,
What of his poorest

That no shadows weep so late in the afternoon?

IV

I printed several of the same paper at the same time,
Feeling each love between its fold.

V

In England a conference at the University of Warwick
Heard a topic on VALUE by Lamarque, where was

Another philosopher present whom two years later
In the capital of Wisconsin would say beside me,

"That's what they always say," about the White Sox.

VI

Cooking inside while snow drifts off the roof
What are these lamps or decorations but excuses?

VII

There is always the idea of someone else's office,
Someone else's measurements and key figures—

Patterns of thought over points of view.

VIII

After some letter each day to Covici is the work of East of Eden,
On the odd page.

He often mentions snapped pencils' tips or the Saturdays
Of too much to have drunk on the other page, what tricks will not work,

There was a way to alternate the story with chapters of letters
And give distinct presence to its families,

Which could be skipped by readers, but this idea
Later was abandoned.

IX

The structure of the play:
Is it always how birds came home to roost?

X

Like a Dane in Den-
Mark the actor's
Eyes,

Night voyages in
A soundless mist.

XI

"O, that my tongue were in the thunder's mouth!"

XII

From exactly 2:04 on Marsilis's "Chambers
Of Tain," 1985

52nd Street NY,
Antique walnut, dark

To 2:25.

XIII

I saw myself walking into
The room, before
It started.

THREE

Sudo Visudo

Pairwi-

Jester Of Frames

▲

The Palm Black

Two-Heated Seat

8415-1-a

Stone Coterie

▲

Livijia

"The properties of
the double city are
well known."

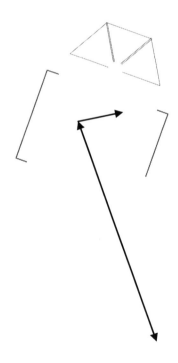

PAIRWI-

There were tables, people didn't have parties.
Also, white sheets

They were not moved to sleep. The braids
Of small trees

  Pulled apart
  S, 2,

The ends risen for the sky.
In the morning

There were tables, people
Didn't have parties. There were not birds

    IN THE BACKYARD
    IN THE BACKYARD

There were clothes
And a gate,

In the mind of the gate
We made

Them carry nothing but their own joy,
And they gave

  Their own joy
  Away to others.

JESTER OF fRAMES

There is no such thing as swim-
Ming. Do
    You link them
In the light in the
    Lanes, some-

        Times sleep on the other side of the bed
    And pre-
        Tend I am you?

THE PALM BLACK

I

A small black shard
  was pulled from my palm,

It stood up
  right on my thumbnail

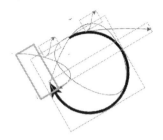

A sharp dimension standing
  over the ridges and pink glow Underneath

The thumb is in fact extension of itself,
  a facet of the fact of my hand

And beyond, the thumb a grouse's bulb
  in my palm,

A bird in my hand, there is a bird in-
  side of my hand.

There is another bird outside
  at the finch station

Their songs together are incorrigible
  facts, like trees

The bulbs of their songs joined
  by the edges along their minds,

The linings and margins, sets, of the trees

flattened underneath

A black shard pulled from my palm.

II

Nature's ovation
  the underbrush'es overture,
    the hanging mannequinne at a foreign cosmic festival

Is that intended direction the first
  thing we ever really do,

These written-on pages, winds
  flipping across the wind

Like a black squirrel, or:
  a sephalange in the dust

A book warped in the heat, or water
  a meditation mill, a round sail bell.

III

Of the world, the beginning of the middle of
  the sea.

There is nightfall in every language.

IV

As it was imagined the day was
  deserted and ancestral

Within that field of colors
  the idea is green rests, rests

Love a series of making moments
  ready for death;

Living a compensation for what
  has been lost;

In divisions where you see
  many of the color

Nights are the charts
  of other nights;

As it was imagined.

V

Folding a paper airplane
  over the sand.

There is your hand
  in every language

Fit with staves in the alternating light.

TWO-HEATED SEAT

AS ONCE ST. JOHN HEARD THE ANGELS
SINGING IN THE HEIGHTS OF HEAVENLY
ZION, NO LESS BEAUTIFULLY AND NOBLY
THE MASS OF ANOTHER GIOVANNI SOUNDS
IN MY EARS. STAY WITH ME NOW UNTIL YOUR END,
PIERLUIGI. LEAD THE SIXTINA DEVOUTLY
FOR ME, AS ONCE FOR THE SAINTLY MARCELLUS!
PRINCE OF THE MUSIC OF ALL AGES! THE SER-
VANT AND SON OF THE POPE

A ball I saw   BAS ↑E ↓KT
  The same lay-
    Up twice

That diner, in
  Fact, is closed, being re-
    Modeled again

I've been (HAVE BEEN) in this
  Spot
    Before, this place

  Light in the kitchen &
    Light in the other room,
      Sewing.

Making the scarf, you can
  Mitzi's eyes grün
    Ashake
      I am walking in

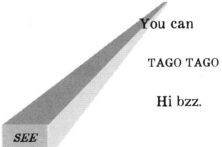

You can

TAGO TAGO

Hi bzz.

SEE

The melodies of all her steps,

8415-1-a

I put

　　A

White hair
　In the middle of a white cand-

Le.

I made a face
　On the swingset,
　　　　W-
　　　　　　here above
The face was made in the pine.

The belief in knowing in the
　fragilis

There, there
　the fragile

Who watches amongst it
all?
　X,

Yes, there it is
　In
　　The wind.

That wild swans
　Make it

There are flowres.

Going well
　The garden,

There are bzz.

Behyond that, behyond
　There's the gate
　　The Gate

　What make me think about
the
　Flowres are

It's a place there has
　A journey
　　Been to most

　The way
Who

Cymbals, duck
　S,

Thinks about bringing them,
The fairness in the flowers,

All those houses in the lily
　Are the garden-bankes

　The good openings
And the final sedu-
　Lousness.

STONE COTERIE

II

And the col-
  Lective spir-
    It in which it was
      Dis-
        Covered and dis-

Cussed,
  A veritable stone
    Gar-
      Den. An

Honomous ex
  It in-
    To the garden; on the
      Roof in the

Sun, the sculptures be-
  Ing re-
    Moved, the sent-
      Ences & — dynamic re-
        Cognizant,

The flash of in-
  Finitum and im-
    Possibility of following
      Curious findings

In-
  To the nest, a lim-
    Inate land-
      Scape having outright

The sun cast her shad-
  Ow in the depths & pos-
    Itives of black.

I

Stone for-
  Gery, cam-
    For, a phosphor

Stone guard absolv-
  Ed as stone man,
    Camphor, a phosphor

Note: the sim-
  Ulacrum, a bridge or bride of neur-
    Al sets, septets of
      Stone nodes fir-
        Ing into the bosom &
observation
          It-
            Self. It is

Good that the most of the
  Set that was writ was
    Shared on a table,
      All of the nodes
        In a quietest fin-

Itude across most
  Of n the fine-
    St tools &
      Methods for organ-
        Izing this tabalature,

LIVIJIA

I'll head over to your spot.
  No two corners,
    A successful room

 We're going to walk
  Down that hall
   Today,

Maybe more like a family room,
  Floors be-
   hind walls they
    Didn't even know existed;

      IT IS RAINING ON THE DINING ROOM
      IT IS RAINING ON THE DINING ROOM

 Table, cyprus
  For pennies a sheet

A bus along a lake
 A square pin,
        sextets, sextinas

 In the reflection
  On the ceiling,

The dining room table,
  Vitrolite

Little fine flying in it,
  Barn-

Swallows, their nest

The limestone has iron
  In it.

  The oak has fallen,
    The birds are still out there.

MAR SON BELLES

A nestle on the partition, engaging the more vague
insights that you can remember, carrying light
and sounds to places way out, and great slow
horses watching the sun, piqued across the
letters in the sky.

A DARK BABY BLUE

And a leaf
   Standing by the wall,
      In fact I took a picture.

THORN IN MY FINGERS

Cats, have you ever found a thorn stick
  In your paw?

Could you direct or specify to me
  Where is it?

Ah, yes   It is there.
  And cats, have you ever found your paw

In a hand, while you sleep?

AN OPEN SPACE MOVES IN
(*Entrammelled*)

A dog with a chest like Tex-
  As,
  His chest like a spell on
    his face, the man
Like a flea, his conjure the cir-
  Cumstance of the faith
    In the circus, of it
The datum of the circus in him
  As it hops ac-
    Coridan like, the circus's scream
Paramita, fire-
  Eaters, common swine and
    Feather-
      Ed sets parked before conjure, before

The learn, before tests were writ
  Before uniterated the dog as his
    Chest was lost.

ST. PATRICK'S DAYE

HAIKU THAT WOULD BE FOUND

SOMEPLACE

NEARBY AN UMBRELLA'D MAI – TAI, 2013

there the sound in the fabric

paper beneath

a coin on the diving board

{ INTERMISSION }

FIVE

A Lillipute Moon

Portrait of H Spect, April <u>MMIX</u>

A Prompt Dependent

Mixed Latencies

Inter-Penitent Quatrefoil

Fysica Quantica ♩ O PASIÓN-SANACIÓN

PORTRAIT OF H SPECT, APRIL MMIX

April, where the doors open, elevator stopped. Blue jacket, denim slacks, gridwork beneath the jacket. The sixth floor of Tapis Hall has its normal three o'clock bodies, overworn and in the tacit motion of only a quarter hour until three, a Wednesday and some weeks before a last seminar on Wittgenstein would end and the last Jastrow duck-rabbit was drawn from the chalk, us watching VHS of a camp English film about Wittgenstein's life Spect found in a used video store in the early nineties in Milwaukee. A long spring conference room and clouds outside and the idea known well by those there that this would be the last meeting like it the scholar would host.

} Nearly very Two, Three years ago today. }

A PROMPT DEPENDENT

On the south of the
Building there is a flag
And it is bound to the sun,
The colors are washed
Unclear and the wind
Is terse or oblique.
Suit-case carried from the
Bus emits the sound of a
RECEIVED
Message . Un –
related, a job will fail
TO –
Night, affecting a series of
Workflows.

On lunchtime downtown
Several block of shadow
Is staged

The taco and Cousins
Ven-
Dor stare at each
Other secretly &
The US Bank building.
Through her doors, spinning,
Discoverers of lunchtime
On Avenue Wisconsin –

49

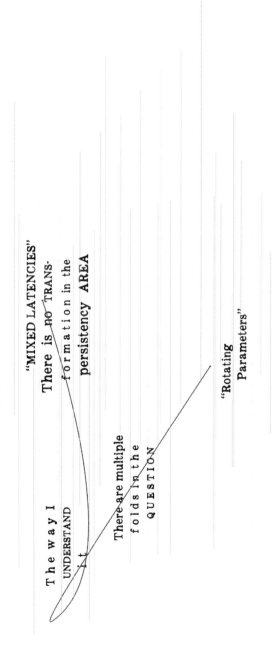

"MIXED LATENCIES"
There is no TRANS-
formation in the
persistency AREA

The way I
UNDERSTAND
it

There are multiple
folds in the
QUESTION

"Rotating
Parameters"

INTER-PENITENT QUATREFOIL

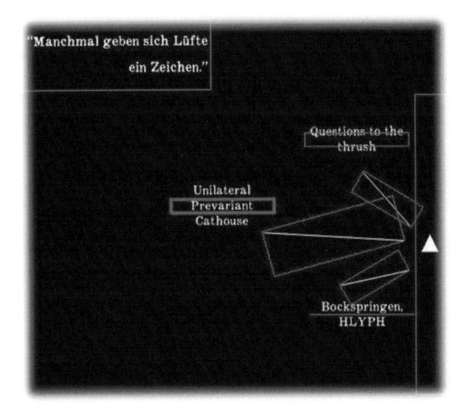

"Manchmal geben sich Lüfte ein Zeichen."

Questions to the thrush

Unilateral Prevariant Cathouse

Bockspringen, HLYPH

FYSICA QUANTICA ⌐ O PASIÓN-SANACIÓN

VI
Gergana,
She cannot give the
The whole book of
The met-

METAMORFOSIS OX-
YGENO

IV
Mechaniisimo
Systeme mechanissimo
Systeme activas mechanissimo
Mas-
Pression el cor
Recto, ex-
Actamundo
Multiplicidad.

III
Lo prende
E variedad.
¿ Lo ves ?

Abrid escuelas y se cerraran cárceles.

Expósito la póema el blanca de loeve;
Es triste ya no ser astrocitos.

II
I am a sea crea-
Ture,
An ocean
Var-
Iation, a
Thrush in the
Lava.

I
Beside the
Black and red chickens, like dinos
Isla, an parada.

SIX

Auxerrois

Two-Phantom Imaging Sample

Trictrac

TWO-PHANTOM IMAGING SAMPLE

1	I
3	
2	An
10	an
2	in
1	is
4	of
1	to
4	
5	And
3	and
2	are
6	has
6	its
1	new
1	old
2	one
4	own
1	set
1	the
1	way
4	
6	Each
2	With
6	each
1	have
2	host
1	poem
1	rest
1	sets

1	wake
4	
1	Each
1	boxes
2	fence
1	final
1	image
2	lower
1	place
1	post;
1	rest.
1	shown
1	value
1	wake.
1	which
2	
1	Each
1	Places
1	colors
2	course
1	hiding
1	image;
1	light;
1	limits
1	poems.
1	stanza
1	sunset
1	though
1	unwake
1	values
1	closure
1	finalis
1	history

2	hundred
2	letters
1	identity
1	property
19	identical
1	mountains
1	assemblage
1	properties.
1	ex-ontolymph
1	Approximation.
1	irreversibility

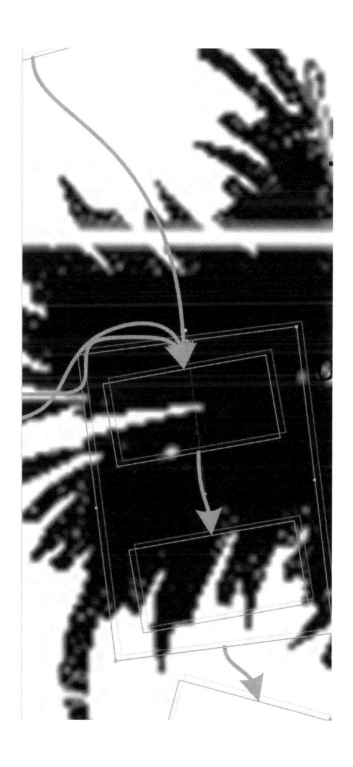

TRICTRAC

S

You want me to work that way.
It's perfect, if

On the morning of a man who
jumps into a window and yells,
"A man jumps from his seat like
he was tripped in a well!"
There is a man who would carry
lumber, with big shoulders
But he would every day catch
himself on the back of his heels
And the wood would scatter
everywhere, and the carpenters
would laugh.

RAMSHACKLE

I SAW HIM ONCE MOVE SOMETHING BEHIND
his back as if he believed, or knew,
THERE WAS NO CHANCE OF IT EVER BE-
ing known that he believed, or knew, he'd moved
THE OBJECT BEHIND HIS BACK AS IF HE BE-
lieved, or knew, there was no chance
OF IT EVER BEING KNOWN THAT HE KNEW HE'D
moved, or that I saw him once move something be-
HIND HIS BACK AS IF HE BELIEVED, OR KNEW,
there was no chance of it ever being know that he
BELIEVED, OR KNEW, HE'D MOVED THE OBJECT
behind his back as if he believed,
OR KNEW, THERE WAS NO CHANCE OF IT EVER
being known that he knew he'd moved, or that I saw
HIM ONCE MOVE SOMETHING BEHIND HIS BACK
as if he believed, or knew, there was no chance of it
EVER BEING KNOWN THAT HE BELIEVED, OR
knew, he'd moved the object behind his back as if
HE BELIEVED, OR KNEW, THERE
was no chance of it ever being known that he knew
HE'D MOVED, OR THAT I SAW HIM
once → move
something
behind
his back as
if he believed,
or knew, he'd moved
the object behind his back
as if he believed, or knew, there
was no chance of it ever being known
that he knew he'd moved, or that I saw him
once ↑ move something behind his back as if he believed,
or knew, there was no chance of it ever being known that
he knew he'd moved or that I saw him once move something behind
his back as if he believed, or knew, there was no chance of it ever be-

You, constantly speaking a language to
your self which you know very little of.

i

i

SEVEN

S / non-S

Four Corners Of Light

[Unknown B]

From Semi-Immaterial To Your Joy

FOUR CORNERS OF LIGHT

The four lights of any corner,
  For the edges,
    The corners of the edges
      Are ghosts, can be,
        Can be-come ghosts,
Reading about ghosts in each cor-
  Ner move-ment, each
    ~~GHAST GASP~~
——Transition as it gasps, each
    Gasp forth, every second
      A gasp, each sound
        In the gasp traced, each
          Moment in the sound
            Be-coming lights
              Traced as a gasp

[UNKNOWN B]

→   IT WAS
      A PLACE YOU'D THOUGHT IT WAS
                BUT WAS-
                   N'T,

      AN EXIT WE'D READ
      ABOUT

    TUNED INTO
        WRIT IN THE MIR-
        ROR

    UNLOCK-
     ED IN THE SENSED DUSTS
       WAVES SHORT
        ENOUGH
          TO OPEN VAWLS
            O U T –

    S I D E THAT
      DO-
        OR, OUTSIDE
          THAT DOOR.

FROM SEMI-IMMATERIAL
TO YOUR JOY

There was always an idea by the gate.
Sometimes the latch stuck through too
far in its lock. Her fingers could call the
latch, just enough space between the door
& the wall.

8

8413

Middle King

"perform bespoke
aggregation"

,

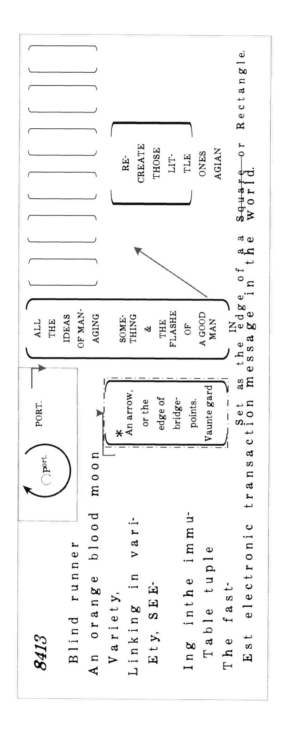

8413

Blind runner
An orange blood moon
Variety,
Linking in vari-
Ety, SEE-
Ing inthe immu-
Table tuple
The fast-
Est electronic transaction message in the world.

PORT.

port.

ALL
THE
IDEAS
OF MAN-
AGING

SOME-
THING
&
THE
FLASHE
OF
A GOOD
MAN

RE-
CREATE
THOSE
LIT-
TLE
ONES
AGIAN

* An arrow,
or the
edge of
bridge-
points.
Vaunte gard

IN as the edge of a a Square or Rectangle.
Set

MIDDLE KING

In the sign there

      is an ar-

Rangement,

The assignment.

Forty three a-

      Ssistants.

A beam lives up-

      Stairs.

      ½ century,

    half vessel

Half of what

  You know −

Half of a shin-

Dig : Half of you don't

Have options after that.

The option of understanding.

A king recreating the king.

"perform bespoke
aggregation"

I'll someday forget
that even there
was a mind. Ifs

↶tether together. He

arrived on time for the meeting,
uninvited.
I have a gratitude
for vertigo. Nothing
about rogue.

The shelf balanced
on the stool

For years, a
way that the small
drawer, oak, the whole
thing was,

Had difficulty in its
frame. No less,

The wallpaper
inside was exact,

Old cards in new
arrangements on the floor
and a little band afar unrestricted from its own awe.

NINE

Ten Control Mills

Orange Blue Green Red

To Log

Facts In Tableau

TEN CONTROL MILLS

In every leg there was
    A storm
  And every foot looked up.
    The storms were
      Low and above the
        Mills, and test-
  Ed the way things were
    Going, be-
      Fore they were
      There.
  Every night each dream
    Was re-
      Membered there
        Was a discussion in the
        Morning.

ORANGE BLUE GREEN
RED

THE ORANGE IS MORE
    PAPERLESS LIKE THE DOOR

    AND A BLUE HANGING
       LIKE A SHEET
          COVERING FOOT TO
            RUNG

      GREEN A BULB

        OR A RED

          OR A RED MY WINDOW

                  [OR A RED
MY WINDOW

TO LOG

THESE POEMS ARE IMPORTANT

    T H I S   H E A T
        Y O U C A N
           N O T   L O G   O N

    TO LOG , TO LOG

      A L L' S   L O S T

        T O   L O G

          AND LO

            THE LOG DOTH
             COMETH IN THE
              POST

FACTS IN TABLEAU

I think birds know
These large machines

In passage in the morning
Are powered by and unlocking

Energy from their giant theropod
Antecedents.

ENSEMBLE CAST, &

E X T R A   P L A Y E R

MOUNTAINS RUN

EAST-WEST

WHICH WAY DID THE WIND BLOW AGAIN ?

TEN

Hurry Up & Wait

55

"The Positional Assignment List

Has Too Many Values"

Ego Vittles

Poem ("audire, muneris")

} From Semi-Immaterial To Your Joy II {

Own Birds

By Oft Predict That

Zookeeper

55

By reading, there are in effect 7700 syllables maintained in Rainer Maria Rilke's 1922 cycle of sonnets "SONNETS TO ORPHEUS" (*Die Sonnette an Orpheus*), written in the same small tower of Muzot and over the same duration as was "THE DUINO ELEGIES" (*Duineser Elegien*). Each poem is composed of 14 (*fourteen*) metrical lines across four stanzas. The first and second stanzas contain four lines and the latter (*latter*) each contain three. Each line approximates to five metrical feet, two metrical syllables per foot. The aggregate work is set by two parts, *n*; the first part stages 26 poems, the second part 29. Each poem's composite syllabary is 140. The division of the number of syllables in the text by this number is 55 (*fifty-five*), the consummate number of poems in the text. If ever you are entrammelled.

Charioteer the scriptures do not
Poet is also an eye.   SEE

EGO VITTLES [

Over the tables where
 Set log\-

Ue of query

  May be found, I began
To

Form the sele] [   ]

Ction that
  Would assemble and re-

Trieve the content, text,
  A query

Using my own id-
  Entity

As a test,
  & found

  The value store-
D in the col-

  Umn of interest
Was the bare string

  Re-
Presenting the SELECT

Statement I'd have just passed

To the corpus,

As a test.

Poem ("audire, muneris")

When asked if you would like a copy of
your receipt
  Hold the unsigned
    Receipt closely <u>&</u>

Along a normal, planned
  Hesitation for capture
    Make a small blink, as if
           snap-

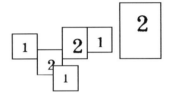

Ping a photograph.

Allow an instant to pass, say no
  Sign the docu-
    Ment

And return it to the Presence
  Retenneting. This

Action appears to have stored the re-
                ceipt
  In your memory, disjoin-

Ing the require-
  Ment of a physical record ; the moderat-

Ing innkeeper of the agree-
Ment in his or her inertness will
understand your

Capability in ado. And perhaps also you
did.

FROM SEMI-IMMATERIAL TO YOUR OWN JOY II

OWN BIRDS

To birds there are other birds
   Back bay birds,
      Birds with other worms

Other gobbles, other trees.
   Other birds with other birdlings;
      Other colors and other little
         Bird music. Other bridges

To fly over, and under high bridges,
   Other buildings and signs, visages, wind-
      posts and other resistentia—
         Daffodils and wishing ponds,
            Peachtrees and new perches.

Bells hanging in the trees, and
   Birdhouses; over birdhouses rock-
      Ing branches and snow white sun,
         Like a nude in the sky, the sun

And why sets of other birds ?

BY OFT PREDICT THAT

}In which to log{
  All the numbers,
There are twelve strokes

  Twelve steps to the stair-
    well, the
      breath helps the
      muscles re-
        member.

    This location, on this
    day,

      Related to the gui-
      dance of
        the stream,

By oft predict that.
  Not
    from the stars
    plucked
  Aged over weathers
    and years, years wed
    about constant stars.

  In which to log all the inv-
    Entions. To jot;

  By oft to predict that.

A long series of inventors.
  Ships in a long series.
    Two, three very even dime's:

They ask
  Only because it seems to
    Happen this way.

ZOOKEEPER

Ledges are common partitions of gravity set by time, keystores to deserialize root structures of the scaled horizon in a distributed consesus of fallover, upswing, net path and display of next options for the ordering and canticles of many next legends.

ELEVEN

Suzuki hamlet

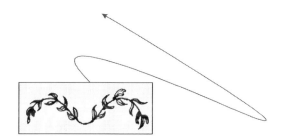

O AS OF YET BUT THAT IT IS A

In the natural de-
  Cay of habit,

The springboard of the billie-
  Goat, twisted

Cranes o' the same neck,

    The outwardness of folk while
      They work iniside together,

    The inwardness while they are
      Outside.

THE FACULTY OR PHENOMENON OF THE WHOLE VAST SECTION OF THE EVE'S COPIED UNKNOWN

Welcome all, good evening summer night,

To 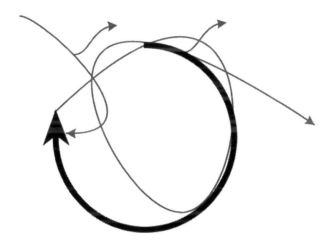's production of In The Belling Stillness, by

Also, welcome you to Tapis Terrace,
Among whose avid gardens, art and architecture

You will have this play tonight.

The   sincerely extends its gratitude for your support of this event,
 Of events past, for you, our patrons, our community

Help build forth what engagements we will have for you in the future.

We are founded on a vision that incorporates local thought, creative mind and collaborative procedures.

It is not without your dear consideration that such a focus could avail.

Are you all very excited ?

Thank you.

The confluence of this space has allowed us to build a play that will move you, veritably,

Through the terrace. The first act takes place here in the courtyard. Thereafter,

A brief intermission will give you the chance to enjoy refreshments in the Great Hall.

Bathrooms are available on the South wing of the building. And also down the side hall and around the corner to the right.

The second act takes place on the upper terrace,
Where the moon may meet us, and after a second
intermission the final act will play on the lower grounds,
overlooking a vast garden,

Where we've laid blankets and set chairs in a slightly, not inperchance as it might be, Arabian setting.

We ask that you kindly observe upon just a few keepings of the house:

IDENTICAL

I have one hundred identical boxes, in which are one hundred
identical poems.
Each stanza in each poem has identical letters,
And each identical assemblage of letters sets an identical
image;
Each identical image has identical colors and new
identical properties.
Each property has an identical set of values,
And each value an identical final light;

Each finalis has an identical course and each closure
an identical rest.
Each rest an identical host,
And each host an identical wake.
Each wake has its own ex-ontolymph,
And each history of its unwake its own
Approximation.

Each identity has its own limits and its own
hiding
Places, though
Each place is identical to an old post;

An identical way the mountains are
shown,
An identical sunset
And its irreversibility,

With an identical lower fence
With an identical lower fence

POEM IN A VELVET COAT

An Partial Non-Unique Index to the Titles of 'TEN CONTROL MILLS'

Line emphasis indicates section title.

na

"audire, muneris", *78*
"rotating parameters", *49*
"the positional assigment
 list has too many values",
 75
 "perform bespoke
 aggregation", *66*
2:25, *21*
55, *74*
<u>8</u>, *63*
8413, *64*
8415-1-a, *31*

A

A DARK BABY BLUE, *37*
A Lillipute Moon, *45*
A PROMPT DEPENDENT, *48*
Adam and Eve
 talking snakes, and, *8*
aliquot, *11*
AN OPEN SPACE MOVES IN, *39*
<u>Åndante</u>, *1*
<u>Auxerrois</u>, *53*

B

berries, *12*
Bhraman Bull, *6*
Billu, *16*
bird, *27*
birds, *3, 17, 21, 25, 34, 71, 81*
birdlings, *81*
BY OFT PREDICT THAT, *82*
bubbles, *4*
bzz, *30-31*

C

Caribbean Sea, *7*
carpenters, *58*
charioteer, *75*
chickens, *52*
city, *24*
cows, *16*

D

Denmark, *21*
disk-player, *9*
dinosaurs, *52*

E

EGO VITTLES, *76*
England, *20*
ensemble cast, *72*
(Entrammelled), 39, 74

F

FACTS IN TABLEAU, *71*
finalis, *55*
FISHING FOR HIDDEN LOONS,
 17
FOUR CORNERS OF LIGHT,
 60
foxes, *15*
FYSICA QUANTICA.. JO , *51*

G

GARY SNYDER'S FIRST
 WALLEYE, *11*
Gergana, *51*

There are approximately one hundred and thirty-two entries in the above guided list.

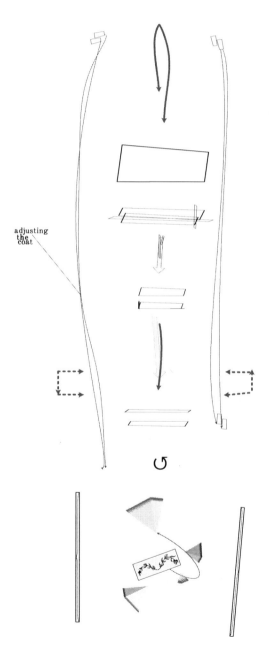

adjusting
the
coat

{ FIN } | TEN CONTROL MILLS

The leading quotation in the frame 'Inter-Penitent Quatrefoil' can be translated as Sometimes breezes give each other a sign, from the work of R. Rilke in the 25th part of Sonnets to Orpheus.

The first poem in the section Auxerrois was produced by a FLATTEN / TOKENIZATION *method on the third poem of the section Suzuki Hamlet using* Pig, *a dataflow scripting language in the Apache Hadoop eco-system.*

Notes and other metadata also available from the author.

Joshua Lickteig holds an M.S. in Management of Information Systems from
the University of Wisconsin-Milwaukee. This is his second book of poetry.
He is active as a senior analyst for a technology organization.

Some of the objects herein were set for print using Visio, by MSFT.

A NOTE ABOUT THE TYPE

This book was set in Appareo.

Designed by K. Kirkwood, the font is a textured worn typeface (an imperfect, worn serif) with varying degrees of impression, weight. It is inspired by the pages of dusty old books, and the beauty of imperfection in the printing process.

Composed by the author, Shorewood, WI.

Deep acknowledgements to my parents & Woodland Pattern Bookcenter.

Special gratitude to Kate Hawley.

Made in the USA
Middletown, DE
04 December 2015